# LIVINGSTONE
## AND THE VICTORIAN
## EXPLORERS

Peter Hepplewhite and Neil Tonge

WAYLAND

# Great Victorians Series

Brunel and the Victorian Engineers
Darwin and the Victorian Scientists
Livingstone and the Victorian Explorers
Owen and the Victorian Reformers

Editor: Carron Brown
Cover designer: Jan Sterling
Designer: Malcolm Walker, Kudos Design
Production controller: Simon Eaton

First published in 1997 by
Wayland Publishers Limited
61 Western Road, Hove
East Sussex, BN3 1JD, England

Find Wayland on the internet at http://www.wayland.co.uk

**British Library Cataloguing in Publication Data**
Hepplewhite, Peter
Livingstone and the Victorian Explorers. – (Great Victorians
Series)
1. Livingstone, David, 1813–1873 – Juvenile literature
2. Explorers – Juvenile literature 3. Discovering geography –
History – 19th century – Juvenile literature
I. Title  II. Tonge, Neil
910.9'22

ISBN 0 7502 2061 9

Typeset by Kudos Editorial and Design Services, England
Printed and bound by G. Canale & C.S.p.A., Turin, Italy

Cover (clockwise from left): Henry Morton Stanley meets
Dr David Livingstone in Ujiji, Africa, 10 November 1871;
Dr David Livingstone; The Victoria Falls, Africa, named
by Livingstone after Queen Victoria.

**Picture Acknowledgements**
The publishers would like to thank the following for allowing
their pictures to be used in this book: Bridgeman Art Library,
London /British Library, London 17 (top); /Mitchell Library,
State Library of New South Wales, Australia 33 (bottom);
National Library of Australia, Canberra 34 (top); /National
Maritime Museum, London 24 (top); /Royal Geographical
Society, London 9; Mary Evans Picture Library 5, 14, 18 (top),
24 (bottom), 27, 34 (bottom); Michael Holford 6; Hulton
Getty 21, 35, 38, 39; Ann Ronan at Image Select 33 (top);
Impact/Colin Jones 7 (bottom); David Livingstone Centre,
Blantyre 10, 12 (middle), 13; By courtesy of the National
Portrait Gallery, London 4, 37; Peter Newark's Historical
Pictures cover [portrait of Livingstone], 8, 12 (top), 20 (both),
23, 26, 28, 29; Popperfoto 25; Science Museum/Science &
Society Picture Library 15; Tony Stone cover [background and
Victoria Falls], /Michael Hoare 7 (top), /Ian Murphy;
Wayland Picture Library cover [Stanley and Livingstone] 11
(bottom), 12 (bottom), 15, 18 (bottom), 22, 30.

Maps on pages 19, 21, 30, 33, 36 and 43 are by Peter Bull.

# Contents

Introduction
A Strange Meeting 4
Chapter One
David Livingstone and the
Quest for the Heart of Africa 10
Chapter Two
Even Deeper into Africa 14
Chapter Three
Search for the Source of the Nile and the Congo 20
Chapter Four
The North-west Passage and the Search for Franklin 24
Chapter Five
Opening a Continent –
Burke and Wills across Australia 31
Chapter Six
Francis Younghusband and the Great Game 35
Chapter Seven
The Legacy of the Explorers 43

Important Dates 45
Glossary 46
Further Information 47
Index 48

# ❧ A Strange ❧ Meeting

There was every reason to believe that David Livingstone was dead. On his fifty-third birthday, 19 March 1866, he had set off from Zanzibar for the unknown interior of Africa. He took with him thirty-six men, his pet poodle, Chitane, and a strange assortment of pack animals: buffaloes, camels, mules and donkeys. Soon some of the men began to fall sick, die or run away. They passed through villages ravaged by slave traders whom Livingstone hated: 'village after village all deserted and strewn with corpses and skulls'.

▼ *This picture shows Livingstone (right) being greeted by Henry Morton Stanley after no one outside Africa had seen Livingstone for four-and-a-half years.*

Despite constant sickness and hunger, Doctor Livingstone went on through leech-infested swamps and burning plains 'every step in pain'. After five years of exploring and mapping, he limped back to Ujiji on the eastern shores of Lake Tanganyika, starving and without supplies. To the world beyond Africa, the good Doctor Livingstone, explorer and missionary, must surely be dead. There had been no sign of him for four-and-a-half years. When Livingstone had reached Ujiji at the lowest point in his fortunes, his faithful servant, Susi, 'came running at the top of his speed and gasped out: "An Englishman! I see him!" and off he ran to meet him'.

# THE DAILY TELEGRAPH, WEDNESDAY, JULY 3, 1872

## DR. LIVINGSTONE'S SAFETY.

## OUTLINE OF HIS DISCOVERIES.

## THE NILE SECRET SOLVED.

We are indebted to the courtesy of the London representative of the *New York Herald* for the following summary of long despatches from Mr. Stanley, the Special Commissioner despatched by that journal in search of Dr. Livingstone.

The American flag at the head of the caravan quickly told of where the stranger had travelled from. Henry Morton Stanley, an ambitious American journalist, born in Wales, had been sent by his newspaper to learn the fate of the greatest Victorian explorer of the day. Such a scoop would not only sell newspapers but, Stanley hoped, bring him fame and fortune. Stanley stepped forward, removed his hat, and said, "'Doctor Livingstone, I presume". "Yes", he [Livingstone] said with a kind smile, lifting his cap slightly, and we shook hands'. For all the formality it could have been a meeting in the heart of Europe or the USA.

The famous meeting at Ujiji on 10 November 1871 is one of the great moments in the history of Western exploration of Africa, the last continental land mass to surrender its secrets.

of rejoicing or excitement. Slowly advancing towards the great traveller, he bowed and said, "Dr. Livingstone, I presume?" to which address the latter, who was fully equal to the occasion, simply smiled and replied, "Yes." It was not till some hours afterwards, when alone together, seated on a goatskin, that the two white men exchanged those congratulations which both were eager to express, and recounted their respective difficulties and adventures.

Mr. Stanley's statement is that Dr. Livingstone appeared to be in remarkably good health, stout and strong, quite undismayed by all that he had gone through, and eager only to finish the task he had imposed upon himself.

▲ *This newspaper article published in 1872 brought news to the British public of Stanley's meeting with Livingstone, reassuring everyone that he was safe and well.*

▶ *In 1443, the ships of Prince Henry the Navigator of Portugal successfully followed the coastline of Africa to find new trade routes.*

Four hundred years before the meeting of Stanley and Livingstone, the first small steps had been taken by Europeans to sail south and explore the African coastline. In 1434, Henry the Navigator, prince of Portugal, sent his ships to follow the coastline and find a sea route to India. This they succeeded in, bringing back a valuable cargo of spices. This was the beginning of European exploration of the continent. The Portuguese were one hundred years behind a Chinese fleet which had sailed to the east coast of Africa, and several hundred years behind the Arabs who sailed regularly to Africa in search of slaves.

Those that followed the Portuguese mapped the coastline – all 30,491 km of it. Gradually, a handful of trading forts and slaving stations peppered the shores. Only the Dutch began to settle in some numbers on the southern tip of the continent. But apart from this sprinkling of Europeans, the map was almost blank from Kuruman in South Africa to Timbuktu in the north.

There were many strange tales told of 'men whose heads did grow beneath their shoulders'. These creatures were never found. There were many other stories about dwarfs, cannibals and even unicorns. These stories turned out to be true, even if the unicorns were proved to be rhinoceroses. The people of Africa were far from being entirely primitive societies. Many of their arts and towns had flourished and fallen – Merowe in Sudan, which had strong ties with Egypt around 500 BC, Benin in West Africa and Great Zimbabwe in East Africa.

Europeans were drawn to Africa through stories of vast wealth. Gold, diamonds and ivory existed in the continent but, up until the late 1800s, the greatest wealth of Africa lay in none of these. The greatest fortunes were made in capturing and selling human beings. Between 1450 and 1880, as many as ten million Africans were sold into slavery. Most African slaves were sent to work in the West Indies and the USA.

▲ Many civilizations flourished in Africa long before Europeans had set foot on the continent. This stone tower is part of the ancient East African settlement of Great Zimbabwe. People lived in the town dating from the 10th–15th centuries.

◄ This great cemetery at Merowe in Sudan dates from around 590 BC.

By 1800, Europeans had discovered the continents of the world. Some of which, like the Americas, they had not known existed previously. At first, they were spurred on by the desire to make riches from trade. They had spread their settlements around the world, convinced that their civilization was superior to all others they discovered.

During the nineteenth century, there was a second wave of exploration and discovery. The interiors of the vast continents of Asia, North and South America, Australia and Africa were unknown. The maps were blank. Fabulous stories of wealth and exotic civilizations cast their spell over Europeans.

There were enormous obstacles to be overcome. Disease, tribal warfare, drought, starvation, deserts, icy wastes, swamps, tropical forests and, above all, the sheer size of the continents. There were no roads or detailed maps. Once explorers left on their journeys they simply disappeared to the world outside. Some re-appeared in two or three years, others vanished – killed, eaten or ravaged by disease.

▼ Explorers faced many new dangers when travelling over wild lands. This picture shows David Livingstone encountering a hippopotamus. It has surfaced from the water, almost capsizing the boat.

What made Europeans, especially British explorers, risk their lives and health in those blank spaces on the map? There is no one answer to this question. Explorers like David Livingstone were driven by their belief in God and their hatred of the slave trade. Some, like Henry Morton Stanley, Richard Burton, John Hanning Speke and many others, were sent by the Royal Geographical Society of Great Britain (founded in 1830) to make maps of the regions they explored. Some went as scientists, like Darwin, to discover new plant and animal life. Burke and Wills crossed the Australian deserts to discover if there was any further land for settlers to farm in the heartlands of Australia. Franklin perished in the Arctic wastes trying to find a route around the north of Canada.

Others dreamed of extending the British Empire ever further. Younghusband marched into Afghanistan and Tibet at the head of an army, even though it was doomed to failure. Many hoped that fortunes could be made from trade. Whatever the motives of explorers, all were convinced that their societies were superior. By imposing their religious beliefs and their values on the countries they explored, they thought they could do good.

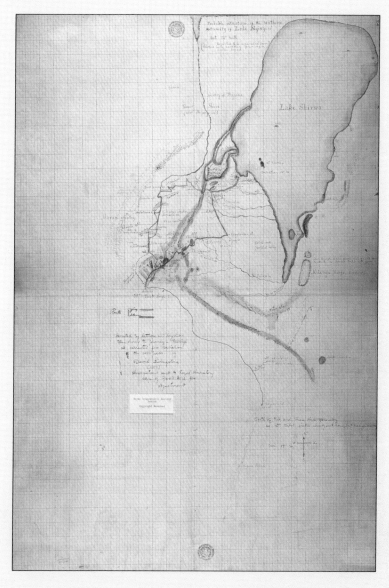

▲ *While Livingstone explored Africa, he drew maps like the one above of Lake Shirwa in Malawi. These drawings were extremely helpful in helping to map out the vast continent of Africa.*

## Chapter One

# ❧ David Livingstone ❧ and the Quest for the Heart of Africa

David Livingstone's hands were icy-blue with the cold. It was a frosty morning, and David was on his way to the cotton mill where he and his parents worked from six in the morning till eight at night. He was only ten years old but he had a huge thirst for knowledge. Propping his books up against the spinning machine he tried to 'catch sentence after sentence' as he worked.

▼ *David Livingstone was born in this room in Blantyre on 19 March 1813. Livingstone shared this single room with his parents while he was growing up.*

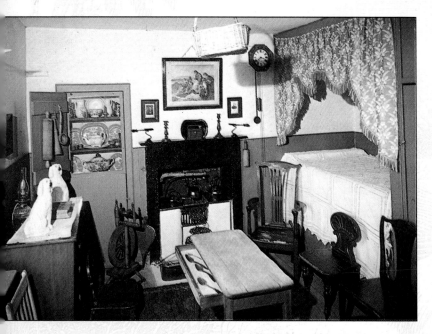

It was this determination to succeed that took David Livingstone from the bleak Scottish village of Blantyre, near Glasgow, where he was born on 19 March 1813, to the scorching plains and forests of Africa as Britain's most famous missionary and explorer. David had great determination and a firm belief in Christianity. David's mother and father were devout Christians and by the time he was twenty years old, he had decided to devote his life to preaching Christianity in foreign lands. At Sunday School, he heard visiting missionaries and the priest weave fascinating tales of strange sights in foreign lands where the word of God was unknown.

Tales of China, particularly, fascinated him, and David vowed that he would preach the gospel just as soon as he was old enough to do so. At the same time, he decided that if he also trained as a doctor, he would be of even more help to the people he wished to convert to Christianity. At twenty years old, David was still working in the mill. He would prop his medicine books up on the spinning machine and read while he worked. Soon he was earning enough in the summer to attend medical classes in Glasgow during the winter and, in 1840, when he was twenty-seven years old, he finally qualified as a doctor.

While at the mission, Livingstone attended a lecture on Africa given by Dr Robert Moffat. At the end of the meeting he asked if there was work for him in Africa. 'Yes,' said Dr Moffat, 'if you are willing to push on to the vast unoccupied district to the north, where on a clear morning I have seen the smoke of a thousand native villages, where no missionary has ever been'. 'Where no missionary has ever been'. The words echoed around Livingstone's mind.

David Livingstone was now ready to start his life's work and journeyed to London as a member of the London Missionary Society. It was at the Society's headquarters that he experienced his first set-back. Britain was at war with China in 1840. This meant it was impossible for him to become a missionary there.

▼ *Livingstone visited villages like Ujiji, in order to teach people about Christianity.*

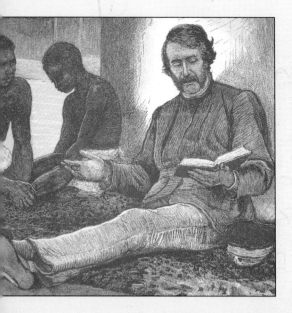

The chance to carry the word of God into unexplored country where no European had travelled before held Livingstone in a spell. In December 1840, he set sail for Africa. The journey took three months and David Livingstone was determined not to waste a minute of his time. He even persuaded the captain to teach him how to use a quadrant – an instrument that enabled sailors to find their exact position at sea. This knowledge was to prove very useful as he was able to make accurate maps of the places he explored in Africa.

▲ *David Livingstone taught the gospels from his Bible, which he carried with him on all his explorations.*

When Livingstone arrived in Africa, he went to the most northerly mission station which was run by his old friend, Dr Moffat. This was at a place called Kuruman and could only be reached after a 1,126-km journey in an ox cart.

▼ *This artist's impression shows Livingstone being attacked by a lion near Mabotsa. Luckily, he escaped being killed.*

◀ *Livingstone's wife, Mary, and their children left Africa for Britain in 1852. Livingstone would return to visit after expeditions. In this photograph taken in 1864, he is with his daughter, Anna-Mary.*

Two years later, Livingstone was drawn further north to start his own mission at Mabotsa. It was here that he nearly lost his life when he was savaged by a lion. Livingstone returned to Kuruman to recover, where he met and fell in love with Robert Moffat's eldest daughter, Mary. They were married in 1845. 'She was,' Livingstone wrote, 'a little, stout, black-haired girl, and all I ask.'

Marriage and children did not curb Livingstone's yearning to see beyond the next horizon and spread the word of God. Mary and David Livingstone set up their mission at Kolobeng, and remained there for five years raising their family.

## Chapter Two

# ∽ Even Deeper ∽ into Africa

Again, the restless desire to preach the gospels persuaded Livingstone to make the hazardous journey of 483 km across the waterless wastes of the Kalahari Desert to reach the lands of the Makololo tribe. The first attempt failed, but a second expedition, in which Mary and their three children accompanied Livingstone, succeeded and they arrived on the shores of Lake Ngami in 1851.

▲ *In 1851, Livingstone and his family reached Lake Ngami. During Livingstone's first explorations, his family would accompany him. In this picture, Livingstone is walking with his son, Robert.*

He felt that somewhere, not very far away, he would find country that could be settled by European farmers. In his companion's words, Cotton Oswell, 'He suddenly announced his intention of going down to the west coast. We were about 1,800 miles [2,896 km] off it. To my repeated objection that it would be impossible he simply replied – "I'm going down. I mean to go down." was the only answer.'

Making his way back to the territory of the Makololo, Livingstone was struck down by malaria, and for the rest of his life he was rarely free from the disease. Whilst he carried little equipment with him – a small tent, a sheepskin cover and a horse rug – he never forgot to take quinine, the best medicine to keep malaria at bay.

David Livingstone was to make three major journeys through Africa. The first of these began in 1852 and took four years. Once again, he crossed the Kalahari Desert to Linyanti, where the young chief, Sekeletu, provided him with twenty-seven men, whose loyalty and stamina proved outstanding. Livingstone's aim was simple and courageous: he would follow the Zambezi River to its source, cross to the west coast, turn around, and follow the river to its mouth on the east coast – a round journey of 8,045 km.

The company travelled by canoe through rivers infested with alligators and hippopotamuses. They took great care for these beasts could easily overturn the canoes. When travelling on the river became too difficult, they travelled on foot. Livingstone reached the coast in just over six months. Returning to Linyanti by the same route, he set off this time to the east coast with his faithful porters.

▲ *One of David Livingstone's most important possessions was his medicine chest. This chest was last used on the journey bringing Livingstone's body back to Britain.*

► *Livingstone wrote about everything he saw on his travels in his dairy.*

In his own diary, Livingstone wrote, 'I at once resolved to save my family from exposure to this unhealthy region by sending them home to England and to return alone, with a view to exploring the country in search of a healthy district that might prove a centre for civilization, and to open up by the interior a path to either the west or east coast.' In April 1852, Mary and the children set sail for Britain leaving Livingstone to seek his destiny.

He had barely started the journey when he came to a halt, marvelling at one of the great wonders of the world. The local Africans called it MOSI-OA-TUN-YA, which means 'the smoke which thunders'. Livingstone decided to christen the waterfall 'The Victoria Falls' in honour of the British queen.

After many adventures, Livingstone reached the Portuguese port of Quilimane on the Indian Ocean. Here the Royal Navy, who were waiting for his arrival, took him aboard ship and brought him back to Britain, the country he had not seen for sixteen years.

▼ *Water thunders down the mighty Victoria Falls. The waterfall is about 104 m in height and 1,400 m wide.*

In Britain he was greeted as a hero. Everywhere he went crowds cheered. Livingstone had become so famous that the government grew interested in his exploits, particularly with the thought that there might be good farming land for European settlers in the heart of Africa. The government granted him £5,000 and a salary of £500 along with men and equipment. Livingstone no longer had to depend on the small sums of money that the London Missionary Society provided.

Livingstone spent much of this money buying a steamboat to sail up the Zambezi River in search of good farming land. Unfortunately, bad luck dogged the expedition. A man less determined than David Livingstone might well have given up. Abandoning the steamboat, Livingstone set off on foot. About 322 km further north he reached the shores of Lake Nyasa, one of the three greatest lakes in Central Africa.

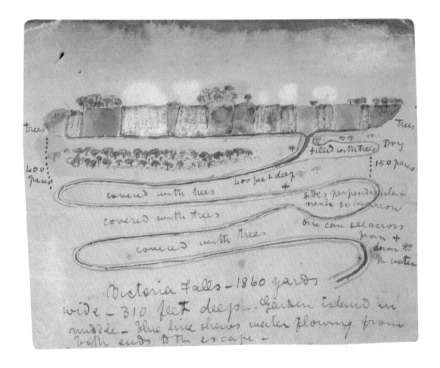

▲ *Livingstone made sketches of what he saw during his explorations. This is his sketch of Victoria Falls.*

It was on this expedition that Livingstone and his men came across a slave caravan surrounded by armed men. Livingstone hated this trade in human beings and attacked immediately. The guards ran away and he was able to free eighty-four slaves. Livingstone's letters home described the full horror of the slave trade. Horrible stories of Arab slavers killing those too tired to walk won sympathy and money from European countries to help end slave raiding. Many of the slaves ended up in Arab countries to the north, but most were exported to the USA to work on the southern cotton plantations.

▼ *Here you can see Stanley's hat (left) and Livingstone's cap (right).*

▲ *This picture shows one of the reasons why Livingstone's navigation of the Zambezi River was difficult. His boat, the* Ma Robert, *has got stuck in mud.*

▼ *After their famous meeting at Ujiji, Stanley and Livingstone explored Lake Tanganyika together by boat.*

Livingstone decided to explore Lake Nyasa next, but to do so successfully would require some sort of boat. Hundreds of Africans were recruited and the boat was hauled hundreds of kilometres overland, until it could be launched from the shores of Lake Nyasa. The sailing boat was not a success. Worse disaster struck. Two Africans, who had joined the expedition later, disappeared one night with the medicine chest. Livingstone now had no quinine to guard him against malaria. Because of this loss, he was stricken with fever. Also, his food supply was running low. He limped back to Ujiji on the east shore of Lake Tanganyika. All his African porters had deserted him, except for the two faithful servants, Susi and Chuma. It was in this desperate condition that he was discovered by Henry Morton Stanley.

Henry Morton Stanley stayed with Livingstone for a further four months. Fresh supplies of medicine quickly restored the missionary's health and together they began to explore the shores of Lake Tanganyika by boat. They hoped to find an outlet from the lake which might prove to be the source of the River Nile. They were greatly disappointed when they found no outlet to the north. At this point, Stanley left Livingstone to go to a hero's welcome in Britain, leaving behind as many supplies as he could.

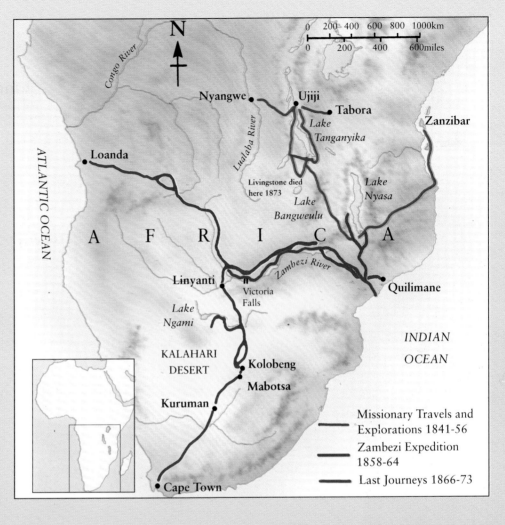

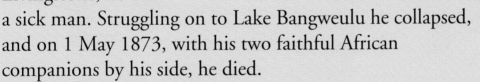

▲ *This map shows Livingstone's explorations in Africa.*

Despite Stanley's description of a lively, healthy Livingstone, he was a sick man. Struggling on to Lake Bangweulu he collapsed, and on 1 May 1873, with his two faithful African companions by his side, he died.

Livingstone is deservedly remembered as the greatest of Victorian British explorers. He had journeyed 46,661 km in Africa and mapped almost 2,590,000 square km. He had discovered six lakes, many rivers and mountains, and the biggest waterfall in the world. But perhaps most important of all, his Christian beliefs had led to further exposures of the evils of the slave trade and helped create a climate in Britain to end the cruel trade throughout the world. In Livingstone's view, only exploration followed by trade and 'civilization' would crush the slave trade.

## Chapter Three

# ❧ Search for the ❧ Source of the Nile and the Congo

Until that famous meeting with Livingstone at Ujiji, Henry Morton Stanley had no thought of exploration.

He had a great determination to succeed that stemmed from his childhood. Born in 1841 the illegitimate son of a Welsh farmer, brought up in a workhouse where he was starved of love and kindness, he became a cabin boy on a ship bound for New Orleans in the USA. Once there, he travelled north and worked as a newspaper reporter for the *New York Herald*. Stanley was asked by the editor of the newspaper to mount an expedition to find Livingstone in 1871. This was Stanley's big chance.

'I detest Africa most heartily', confessed Stanley in his diary. 'I am seldom well except for a day or two when steeped in quinine.' He soon found himself, however, as famous as the good doctor he had discovered and was asked to continue Livingstone's explorations in the search for the source of the River Nile. Stanley took up the challenge with three clear objectives in mind. He wished to sail around Lake Victoria and then Lake Tanganyika to discover if there was a river outlet to the north. Lastly, he wanted to reach the Lualaba River where Livingstone had abandoned it and follow it to wherever it led. To achieve his first two targets he bought a barge – the *Lady Alice*. She could be taken apart in five sections and carried to the lakes to be re-assembled.

▲ The *Lady Alice* was used by Stanley and his men to travel down the River Congo.

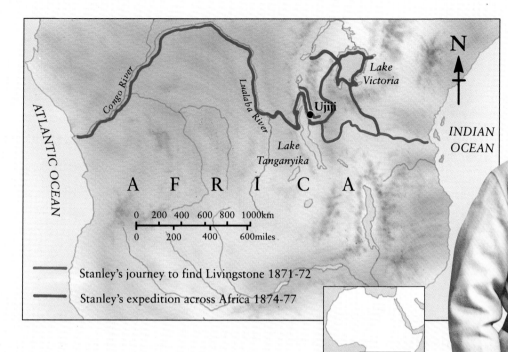

Stanley's journey to find Livingstone 1871-72

Stanley's expedition across Africa 1874-77

Despite setbacks, Stanley reached Lake Victoria and set sail for the northern shore.

After both lakes were explored and proved that they could not be the source of the River Nile, Stanley set upon his third target. Travelling the length of the Lualaba River proved more difficult. His company suffered from starvation, dysentery and smallpox, and was often under attack from cannibals who saw Stanley and his men as fresh meat. Every day, two or three dead bodies had to be thrown overboard from their canoes.

On 12 August 1877, exactly 999 days after their departure, they reached the mouth of the Congo River. Stanley had 'drawn in' another valuable part of the map of the interior of Africa. This satisfied Stanley. He was famous. The following year he married in Westminster Abbey in London, bought a country estate in Surrey and was knighted. The workhouse boy had come a long way.

▲ *Sir Henry Morton Stanley in the clothes he wore during his explorations.*

One of the strangest tales in Victorian times involved a bitter disagreement between two explorers – Richard Burton, a brilliant army officer who had mastered dozens of languages, and his companion, John Hanning Speke. After their attempt to find the source of the River Nile they fell out. Speke was convinced he had discovered the source of this most important river. Burton disagreed. A debate was arranged to take place at Bath in September 1864 when the matter would be settled. As Burton waited for Speke's arrival, a messenger arrived and whispered in his ear. Speke had died of gunshot wounds that morning when his gun had been accidentally fired whilst hunting. Burton and others thought otherwise. Had Speke killed himself to avoid the humiliation of being proved wrong by Burton?

▼ *Speke and Grant speaking in front of the Royal Geographical Society about their dispute. Livingstone was asked to judge the debate in Bath that never took place.*

◀ *Sir Samuel and Lady Florence Baker discovered Lake Albert in Africa, in 1864.*

A husband and wife team also set out to discover the source of the River Nile. Samuel Baker was the son of a wealthy shipowner who led the life of a rich Victorian gentleman explorer. His beautiful wife, Florence, shared her husband's love of adventure. 'Mrs Baker was not a screamer', claimed her husband. It was just as well. Deciding to sail down the River Nile, they were determined to attack the problem from this direction rather than setting out across central Africa. On 18 December 1862, the Bakers set sail from Khartoum in three boats loaded with provisions. Their most difficult moment occurred when an African king demanded Baker's wife. Baker pointed his pistol at the king, 'If this was to the end of the expedition then it would also be the end of the king.' Fortunately it did not come to this and the couple were released. They journeyed on and, after many disasters, discovered a large lake which the Bakers named Lake Albert, in honour of Queen Victoria's husband. Whilst it was not the true source of the Nile, it placed another important piece in the jigsaw map of Africa.

## Chapter Four

# The North-west Passage and the Search for Franklin

▲ *This portrait shows Sir John Franklin painted in his Royal Navy uniform.*

▼ *Franklin's ships, the* Erebus *and the* Terror, *were two of the strongest and best-equipped vessels ever sent to the Arctic.*

In 1845, the year Livingstone married in the tropical heat of Africa, Captain Sir John Franklin and 129 men set for the ice-choked waters of the Arctic. They set sail in two strong ships, the *Erebus* and the *Terror,* but never returned. What had happened to the Franklin expedition? The reputation of the Royal Navy rested on finding the answer.

In 1850, a fleet of twelve rescue ships searched the cold dangerous waters. At the end of August, the first evidence was found. It did not look good. On the bleak shore of Beechy Island, a search party spotted a camp site. There were no messages to be found but the camp told its own story. In the light of the midnight sun, three tombstones cast their eerie shadows. They were dated between January and April 1846. On the grave of John Torrington the inscription read that he had died 'on board her Majesty's ship *Terror*'. This showed that Franklin's men had managed to survive their first bitter winter and that at least one ship had still been afloat.

A tall cairn made out of about 700 large, tinned meat cans worried the rescue party even more. These tins of food should have lasted the men far longer than one year. A grim guess was that the cans had let air inside and the meat had rotted. Franklin's sailors had checked the cans and opened them, building a forlorn memorial to their shrinking food supplies. Finally, there were signs that the camp had been abandoned in a hurry, including a pair of officer's cashmere gloves set out to dry and left behind. But where had the other members of the company gone? After five years, could there be any hope of finding survivors?

Of all the Victorian explorers, none were braver than those who challenged the Arctic. This vast area around the North Pole is one of the most cruel surfaces on Earth. Yet since the 1600s, British sailors had been struggling to find a new trade route around the top of Canada to the spice-rich countries of the Indies. This was the quest for the fabled North-west Passage.

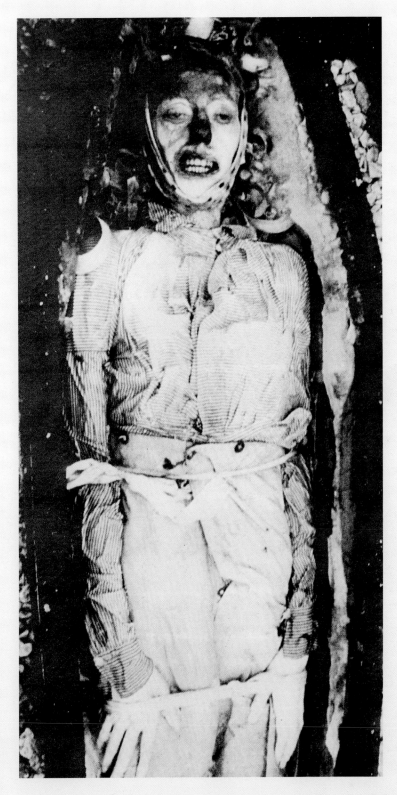

▲ *The 138-year-old body of petty officer John Torrington was photographed by Canadian archaeologists in 1984. The bitter Arctic temperatures had freeze-dried his corpse.*

On modern maps it looks easy: from Baffin Bay, through Lancaster Sound, Barrow Strait, Melville Sound and out into open water through McClure Strait. But the maps are misleading, as these are not ordinary seas. During winter, the waters are locked deep in ice. During the brief summer, a thaw brings a mass of narrow channels clogged with ice floes, and hidden by frost, smoke and fog.

By 1700, repeated attempts to find a way through this maze had failed. It was clear that any route would be so dangerous that it was not worth risking ships and their cargoes. But a century later, other motives besides trade inspired a new generation of explorers. British scientists clamoured to know more about this awesome region and the Royal Navy was eager to take up the challenge. The most powerful fleet in the world wanted the glory of finding the North-west Passage.

From 1818, the great age of British polar exploration began. A group of Navy officers including John Ross, James Clark Ross, William Edward Parry and George Back led the attack on the Arctic and became national heroes. At the front of their ranks was a friend and keen rival, John Franklin.

▼ *Franklin's overland expeditions made him famous. This artist's impression shows him taking observations for map-making at Great Bear Lake.*

During two overland expeditions in 1819–22 and 1825–7, Franklin's teams successfully mapped 3,218 km of the Alaskan/Canadian coastline. Their adventures were hair-raising. In 1821, food was so short that they were forced to make soup from boiled deerskins and old bones. They were only saved from starvation by Canadian Indians.

In 1826, Franklin's boats were attacked by knife-wielding Eskimos. Bravely, he gave the order not to open fire and to allow them to take what they wanted. This risk paid off when most of the stolen goods were brought back. On his return, Franklin was knighted and rewarded with the post of governor of Van Dieman's Land, now called Tasmania.

In 1843, Sir John begged for one last crack at discovering the North-west Passage. When Lord Haddington, First Lord of the Admiralty, suggested he was too old at sixty, Franklin protested: 'No my lord you have been misinformed, I am only fifty-nine'.

▲ *The Franklin mystery gripped the Victorian public. There were no survivors from the Franklin expedition to tell exactly what had happened, so artists imagined scenes from the voyage. This picture shows* Erebus *and* Terror *moving through the frightening beauty of the Arctic.*

Franklin was delighted when he was given command of two of the strongest and best-equipped ships ever sent to the Arctic. Their bows were reinforced with iron sheets and their holds packed with enough supplies for three years. The *Erebus* alone carried 35 tonnes of flour, 24 tonnes of meat and almost 2 tonnes of tobacco. Cleverly, she had an emergency power unit, a 15-tonne locomotive adapted to drive a 2-m propeller. If the ice was not too thick, she could ram her way through.

On 19 May 1845, the Franklin expedition left Britain and was last seen by a whaling ship on 22 July in Disko Bay. Then the long silence began. For two years no one worried. It was routine for Arctic explorers to be out of touch. In 1848, the first rescue vessels set out on a fruitless search. Even the sad finds of 1850 did not mark a breakthrough and one rescue ship, the *Investigator*, commanded by Captain Robert McClure, was trapped in the ice for three years. In May 1853, the desperate crew came close to starving and had to abandon the *Investigator*, trudging 321 km across the frozen sea to be rescued.

▼ The Terror *had been to the Arctic before, under the command of Captain George Back in 1837. This scene shows her 'nipped' or trapped in the ice.*

▲ *An artist's impression of the death of the last survivors of the Franklin expedition – from cold, starvation and exhaustion.*

After this lucky escape, the Royal Navy gave up the hunt for Franklin, but his wife, Lady Franklin, did not. She paid £20,000 towards the cost of fitting out a small steam yacht, the *Fox*. In 1857, the *Fox* set out under Captain Leopold McClintock to follow new clues. Eskimos had reported that a large party of white men had died dragging heavy sledges off King William Island. Struggling to stay alive some had eaten the flesh of the dead.

It took two years of hard searching before McClintock's men found the final proof of Franklin's fate. In a stone cairn at Point Victory on King William Island, they found a brass box. Inside, in tiny scrawled handwriting, was the Franklin expedition's last message (*see* box to the right).

As the Eskimos had seen, they did not get far.

' *25* April 1848 … Erebus *and* Terror *deserted on 22 April, 5 leagues NNW of this, having been beset [trapped] since 12 September 1846 … The officers and crew … 105 souls landed here in Lat. 69 37' 42", Long. 98 41'. Sir John Franklin died on 11 June, 1847. Start tomorrow for Back's Fish River.*'

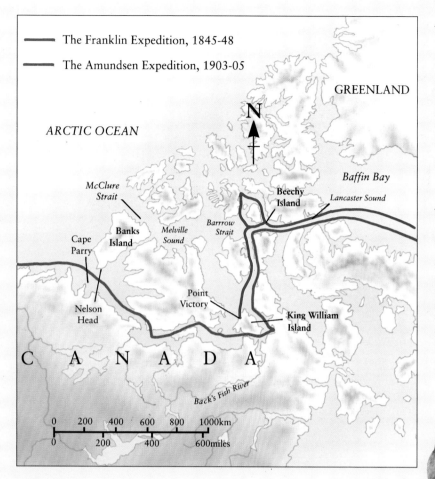

The Franklin Expedition, 1845-48

The Amundsen Expedition, 1903-05

*ARCTIC OCEAN*

GREENLAND

*McClure Strait*

Banks Island

Cape Parry

Nelson Head

*Melville Sound*

*Barrrow Strait*

Beechy Island

*Lancaster Sound*

*Baffin Bay*

N

Point Victory

King William Island

C A N A D A

*Back's Fish River*

| 0 | 200 | 400 | 600 | 800 | 1000km |
| 0 | 200 | | 400 | | 600miles |

When the *Fox* returned with its bitter news, Franklin was proclaimed a national hero and a monument was raised to him in London. It boldly declared he had completed 'the discovery of the North-west Passage'. This claim was disputed for years by other explorers and other countries. His ships, they argued, might have found the beginning of a way through the Arctic but they did not finish it.

Whatever the claims and counter-claims, Franklin's bravery and sacrifice became an inspiration. One young Norwegian boy who read his story keenly was Roald Amundsen. It convinced him that he too should challenge the Arctic. In 1903, aged thirty, he set out with a crew of six men in a converted fishing boat, called the *Gjoa*. After surviving two winters trapped in the ice, they sailed between Cape Parry on the Canadian mainland and Nelson Head on Banks Island. Amundsen had led the first complete crossing of the North-west Passage.

▶ *The Norwegian explorer Roald Amundsen was captain of the first ship to sail the North-west Passage.*

## Chapter Five

# ❧ Opening a ❧ Continent – Burke and Wills across Australia

The first European settlers in Australia arrived unwillingly in January 1788. They were convicts shipped out by the British government. Yet within sixty years, this huge island continent had changed from a dumping ground for criminals into a group of thriving colonies of the British Empire. Although the coastline of Australia had been mapped by Matthew Flinders in 1801–3, little was known about the rest of the vast and empty country. Gradually, explorers began to open it up.

In 1840, Yorkshireman John Eyre pushed east from Adelaide to Albany, a trip of 2,500 km, on foot. In 1844, Charles Sturt got within 350 km of the centre of Australia before being driven back by lack of supplies and oncoming blindness. At the same time, the German Ludwig Leichhardt travelled north from Brisbane to Darwin, over 5,000 km. The reports of these brave men were disappointing. Much of Australia seemed to be a sun-scorched, harsh world.

▼ There were about 300,000 native aborigines when white settlers first came to Australia. This painting gives an old-fashioned view of brave explorers driving off hostile natives. In reality, settlers treated many aborigines badly and they began to fight back.

In 1851, the discovery of gold brought a stream of immigrants who wanted their own farmlands. At the same time, Australia needed to find a route for a transcontinental telegraph line to link up with an undersea cable from India and the rest of the world. With this in mind, the Royal Society of Victoria raised £15,000 to pay for a fifteen-man expedition from Melbourne to the Gulf of Carpenteria. It was the most expensive and best-equipped of its kind.

▲ *The people of Melbourne cheer Burke and Wills as they set off in 1860. The cavalcade of camels was a treat for the crowd.*

Camels were bought instead of horses, as they survive better in the desert. Six came from a local circus and another twenty-five were specially imported from India. Around 21 tonnes of supplies included preserved food, rifles, four pairs of boots for each man, twelve tents and four dozen fishing lines. The main problem was the choice of leaders. Robert O'Hara Burke was a forty-year-old Irishman from Galway, an ex-soldier and a policeman. The expedition surveyor, John Wills, was twenty-seven, a meteorologist from Melbourne. Neither man was an experienced explorer.

▲ *Robert O'Hara Burke (1820–61) was the leader of the tragic 1860 expedition to cross Australia.*

They set out amidst cheering crowds on 20 August 1860, but winter rains slowed them down and they had only reached the small settlement of Menindee by mid-October. Burke began to make mistakes. He split the expedition into two and pressed on over 600 km of flat, empty country to the next source of water at Coopers Creek. Leaving William Brahe in charge of the camp, he split the party again, striking out on 16 December for the Gulf of Carpenteria.

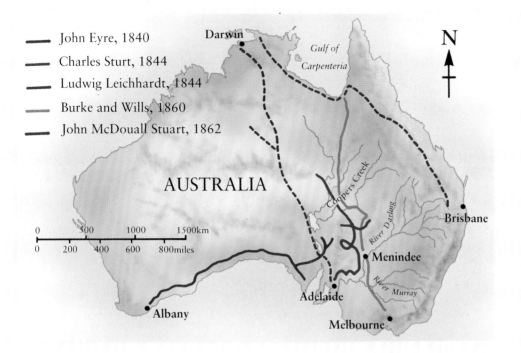

John Eyre, 1840
Charles Sturt, 1844
Ludwig Leichhardt, 1844
Burke and Wills, 1860
John McDouall Stuart, 1862

N

AUSTRALIA

Darwin
*Gulf of Carpenteria*
Coopers Creek
River Darling
Brisbane
Menindee
River Murray
Adelaide
Albany
Melbourne

0    500    1000    1500km
0  200  400  600  800miles

*This map shows the routes of exploration across Australia between 1840–62.*

This time he chose just three companions, John Wills, Charles Grey and John King. At first all went well. On 10 February 1861, they joyfully accomplished their mission, battling through mangrove swamps to reach the northern coast of Australia. But now the problems began. They were exhausted, running out of supplies and had to get back.

The return journey was a nightmare. Endless rain churned their path into treacherous mud. They had no tents, slept in the wet and, as rations ran low, became ill with scurvy. By 30 March, they were very weak and had killed and eaten three of their precious animals.

On 17 April, Grey died and the others barely had the strength to dig him a shallow grave. Four desperate days later, they staggered into the Coopers Creek camp, only to find it empty. Carved into a tree they read 'Dig 3ft NW 21 April 1861'. When they dug down they found a box with food for a month and a note. Brahe and the others had given them up for lost and left – that very morning.

Wills and King wanted to chase after Brahe, but Burke persuaded them to travel across the outback for a settlement at Mount Hopeless, 241 km to the south. By 17 May, they had eaten all of their supplies, only surviving with the help of local aborigines who fed them cake made with nardoo seeds and fat rats. They then headed back to Coopers Creek, hoping to find a rescue party. In fact, Brahe had returned on 8 May, but he had not checked to see if the buried supplies had been touched. He left again without knowing he was only a few kilometres from the stricken men.

▼ *Burke hoped to reach help by heading for a settlement at Mount Hopeless, but by then his party were too weak to survive.*

Burke and Wills died around 30 June, but King was kept alive by aborigines until a rescue party found him on 18 September. Grim, bad luck had led to disaster but, like Franklin before them, Burke and Wills had set a heroic example for others. In July 1862, a second expedition led by John McDouall Stuart reached the shores of the Indian Ocean at Darwin and made it back safely to Adelaide.

## Chapter Six

# ❦ Francis Younghusband ❦ and the Great Game

▲ *Sir Francis Younghusband (1863–1942) photographed in 1895.*

▼ *The magnificent Himalayas lit up by the evening sun.*

In 1903, India was the jewel in the crown of the vast British Empire. But all was not well. The northern borders of India were the playing fields of the Great Game, where the Russian Empire and the British Empire were rivals for control of the area. The British viceroy, Lord Curzon, was sure that the Russians were ready to strike in Tibet and threaten the safety of India. Alarmed, Curzon decided to make a show of British strength. He had just the man in mind, Francis Younghusband, explorer, cavalry officer and the son of a general.

Younghusband had first arrived in India in 1882, a keen soldier of nineteen. His earliest taste of the Indian frontier came in 1884 when he spent two months touring the Himalayan mountains. One freezing night, he sheltered in the high Rhotang Pass. After a bleak meal of cold tinned kippers, he went for a walk and saw a sight which changed his life: 'One peak after another was lit up till at last the moon rose on the whole valley. The air was clear like crystal; the snowy whiteness of the mountains glowing with a holy radiance.'

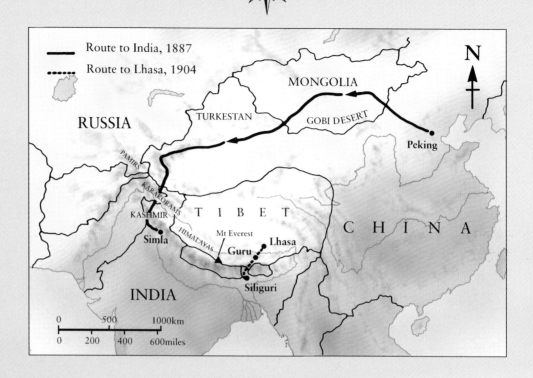

► Younghusband's expeditions in 1887 and 1904.

▼ Mohamed Tsa was Younghusband's guide on his expeditions through Tibet and Central Asia.

This convinced Younghusband that he must become an explorer. He learned the skills of mapping and surveying, and persuaded the army to use him as a scout, roaming Central Asia to look for signs of Russian meddling. In April 1887, he set out on the epic journey that made him famous. It took him from Peking across the wastes of the Gobi Desert, on through the mountains of Turkestan and across the mighty Karakorams to rejoin his regiment in India – over 3,218 gruelling kilometres.

Crossing the Gobi Desert was full of risk. During the day, his small party had to shelter from the scorching sun, only riding their camels from 3 p.m. until midnight. Their old guide, an opium addict, could ride while he was sound asleep. Younghusband wrote: 'As night fell he would suddenly wake up, look at the stars to tell the time, and then as at much of the country as he could see. After a while he would turn the camel off the track and sure enough we would find ourselves at a well.'

When the rains came, the desert became a sucking and heaving swamp. The camels stuck fast and had to be beaten and dragged on to small gravel hillocks. At times, sand and gravel storms ripped through the air forcing them to lie flat until the wind dropped. The last hundred kilometres were the worst. 'Nothing we had passed hitherto can compare with it – a succession of gravel ranges without any sign of life, animal or vegetable, and not a drop of water.' Desperately thirsty they finally reached farmland and saw their first house for 1,609 km. Their desert ordeal was over and they drank until they were ready to burst.

Over the next ten years, the Indian government ordered Younghusband to explore the mountain ranges of the north-west frontier. He risked danger mapping remote passes and bargaining with tribespeople who hated British power. However, his one great wish was blocked. His plan to sneak into Tibet disguised as a native trader was repeatedly turned down. If he was discovered, this would cause a row with Russia. When Curzon sent for him it was the answer to his dreams.

▼ *Younghusband (second from the right) tired and exhausted after trekking through the mountains.*

## FEARS FOR A SECRET LAND

Lack of knowledge about Tibet made Lord Curzon's fears worse. Fabulous stories were told about golden temples and flying monks. However, facts were few. The Lamas, or Buddhist monks who ruled Tibet, had successfully kept out Europeans and modern ideas. Yet by 1903, it seemed they had taken sides.

Curzon had grim news that a Russian secret agent, Arguan Dorijev, was at work in Lhasa, the capital of Tibet. Rumours claimed that he was teaching the young Dalai Lama. Worse still, the Dalai Lama had sent him on several visits to the Russian Tsar. In reality, it was doubtful if either the Dalai Lama or the Tsar took Arguan seriously. Unluckily for Tibet, Lord Curzon did.

◀ *George Curzon, Viceroy of India, who feared that the Russians wanted to take over Tibet and threaten British rule in India.*

When Younghusband finally set out for Tibet, he was escorted by 1,150 soldiers and two maxim guns. This was exploration by force. The huge supply train was carried by 10,000 tribesmen and thousands of mules, bullocks and yaks. There were even two 'zebrules'. These animals were half-mule and half-zebra. Sadly, as the expedition climbed to the icy passes of the Himalayas, mountain torrents, disease and landslides killed many of the animals.

When the British crossed into Tibet in December 1903, they were met by Tibetan officials who refused to let them through. The Tibetans vowed that Europeans, Russian or British would never be allowed in the Tibetan capital of Lhasa. For two months, the British waited in terrible conditions. The *Daily Mail* journalist with Younghusband's company wrote: 'A driving hurricane made it impossible to light a fire or cook food. Twenty men of the mule corps were frostbitten and there were seventy cases of snow blindness among the Gurkhas.'

◀ *A picture from* The Graphic *magazine, 30 January 1904, showing the gruelling British march into Tibet.*

▲ *British troops open fire with their modern weapons and massacre Tibetan warriors. An illustration from* The Graphic *magazine, 30 April 1904.*

On the 31 March, the British advanced a further 16 km towards Guru, where they were met by 2,000 Tibetan warriors. According to Younghusband, his men surrounded them and began to disarm the Tibetans. As this was going on, shots were fired by warriors who refused to give up their guns. According to Tibetan sources, the British persuaded the warriors to put out the lighted fuses on their old-fashioned muskets – making them useless – and then treacherously opened fire.

Whatever the facts, the result was a massacre. The British guns tore through the Tibetan army and over 700 men were killed. 'I got so sick of the slaughter', wrote one officer, 'that I stopped firing even though the order was make as big a bag as possible.'

When Younghusband's force marched into Lhasa on 3 August 1904, the total number of Tibetans killed was 2,500 against only forty British deaths.

Reaching Lhasa was the greatest moment of Younghusband's life. 'The goal of so many travellers' ambitions was actually in sight … The sacred city so far and deep behind the Himalayan ramparts, and so jealously guarded from strangers was before our eyes.'

But he was soon a disappointed man. To his deep regret, there were no Russian troops to drive out, no sign of the Russian secret agent, Arguan Dorijev, and the Dalai Lama had fled. Outside of the temples, Lhasa was a filthy and depressing city.

▼ *This photograph shows British troops marching into Lhasa in 1905, a year after they had taken the city by force.*

► *Lhasa today with its spectacular surroundings is now under Chinese rule.*

Younghusband made the Tibetans agree to sign a treaty containing many harsh terms, including opening their borders with India to trade and paying £50,000 towards the costs of the British invasion. Yet while the British people and papers praised him, the British government was annoyed. The treaty he had forced on Tibet was too hard. This gave other countries a good reason to accuse Britain of being a bully and demand changes. Finally in 1906, Britain and Russia agreed to end the Great Game and allow China to have the biggest say about what happened in Tibet.

Francis Younghusband was given a knighthood but his great days of leadership and exploration were over. For a time he became the British representative in Kashmir. He turned to writing and gained an interest in eastern religions. He died in 1940. The Younghusband expedition had been the last great adventure of the Victorian age.

## Chapter Seven

# ❦ The Legacy ❦ of the Explorers

Davidavid Livingstone was quite clear what exploration would lead to: 'After the work of exploration comes the harder task of civilization.' For missionaries such as Livingstone, this meant the teaching of Christianity, the end of the slave trade and peace between peoples. Unfortunately, not all British and Europeans had the same idea. Mapping the heartlands of continents left them open to aggressive European powers that wanted to conquer and control these newly mapped territories. There were some good effects. Led by Britain, the slave trade was ended. But in some parts of Africa, European influence was very cruel.

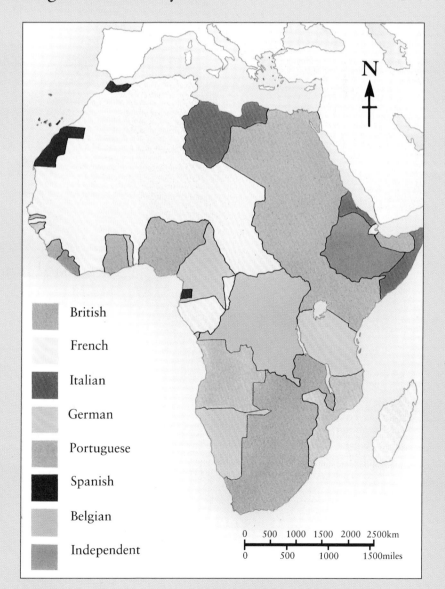

British

French

Italian

German

Portuguese

Spanish

Belgian

Independent

0   500  1000  1500  2000  2500km

0        500       1000      1500miles

▶ *This map shows the African colonies in 1900. All of Africa, except for Abyssinia, was controlled by British and European powers.*

► *European exploration and colonization was sometimes very cruel to the African natives. The slave trade was one of the most cruel aspects, with many Africans being shipped to the USA and the West Indies.*

▼ *Nelson Mandela became the first black president of South Africa in 1995, creating equal rights for everyone in the country for the first time.*

Worst of all, exploration brought conquest. From 1880 onwards, there was a desperate rush by European countries to grab huge territories in Africa and in other continents of the world. Britain led the way. By the early part of the twentieth century, Britain controlled nearly one-quarter of the world's land surface, held together by the biggest single fleet of ships in the world.

Ninety years later, British and European control of the world had slipped away. Empires that had stretched over the globe had crumbled and fallen away as peoples throughout the world took control of their own countries. By the end of the twentieth century, the last country where a small, European population ruled over a majority of Africans had given way.

# IMPORTANT DATES

1434   Prince Henry the Navigator of Portugal sends his ships to explore the coast of Africa.

1652   First European settlers from the Netherlands arrive at the Cape of Good Hope, South Africa.

1788   First European settlers arrive in Australia.

1813   David Livingstone is born.

1840   Livingstone arrives in Africa.

1842   Livingstone begins a mission station at Mabotsa.

1845   Livingstone marries the daughter of the missionary Robert Moffat. Captain Sir John Franklin leads an expedition to the Arctic to try to find the North-west Passage.

1847   Sir John Franklin dies on board the ship *Terror*.

1848   Last survivors of the Franklin expedition die. The first rescue ships are sent out, not knowing that it was already too late.

1849   Livingstone crosses the Kalahari Desert.

1850   First graves of the Franklin expedition found on Beechy Island.

1853   Richard Burton makes a secret trip to Mecca in Saudi Arabia.

1855   Discovery of the Victoria Falls by Livingstone.

1857   Final proof of the death of Franklin's men found on King William Island.

1859   Discovery of Lake Nyasa by Livingstone.

1860   Speke and Grant's expedition to find the source of the River Nile. Burke and Wills set out to find the transcontinental route across Australia.

1861   10 February  Burke and Wills reach the northern coast of Australia. 21 April  Burke and Wills return to deserted camp at Coopers Creek. Around 30 June, Burke and Wills die from exhaustion, illness and starvation.

1862   The Bakers expedition sets off to find the source of the White Nile. John McDouall Stuart makes first return south to north crossing of Australia.

1865   The Bakers return safely to Khartoum.

1871   The famous meeting between Henry Morton Stanley and David Livingstone at Ujiji.

1873   Livingstone dies and his body is brought back to Britain for burial in Westminster Abbey, London.

1877   Henry Morton Stanley's expedition arrives at the mouth of the River Congo after three years exploring.

1887   Francis Younghusband crosses the Gobi Desert.

1891   *The Times* falsely reports that Younghusband is killed by Russians.

1903–5   Amundsen finds the North-west Passage.

1903–4   Younghusband leads the invasion of Tibet. Enters Tibet's capital city, Lhasa, on 3 August, 1904.

# GLOSSARY

**Aborigines**  The native people of Australia.

**British Empire**  Lands conquered and ruled by the British.

**Cairn**  A man-made mound of stones that acts as a marker.

**Cannibals**  People who eat people.

**Caravan**  A group of people travelling together.

**Cavalry**  A group of soldiers on horseback.

**Creek**  Stream or small river.

**Dalai Lama**  The ruler of Tibet. The leading monk and king.

**Devout**  Very religious.

**Dysentery**  A very infectious disease that causes terrible diarrhoea.

**Epic**  Grand or heroic.

**Frontier**  The border between two countries.

**Frostbitten**  When the flesh becomes frozen and damaged.

**Gospels**  The teaching of Christianity, or one of the works in the Bible that tells us about the life of Christ.

**Great Game**  The rivalry between Britain and Russia in Central Asia.

**Gurkhas**  Fierce soldiers from Nepal who fought for the British. There are still Gurkha regiments today.

**Illegitimate**  A baby born to parents who are not married.

**Knighthood**  Given the title 'Sir' by the monarch.

**Lat.** (short for latitude)  Grid lines running across the globe to help sailors find their destination.

**Long.** (short for longitude)  Grid lines running down the globe to help sailors find their destination.

**Malaria**  A disease spread by the bite of an insect called a mosquito.

**Mangrove**  A type of tree.

**Maxim gun**  An early form of machine gun. It could fire bullets quickly.

**Meteorologist**  Someone who studies the weather.

**Mule**  A cross between a male donkey and a female horse. They are very strong.

**Musket**  A gun with a long barrel fired by the spark from a flint. It was a very poor weapon compared to a British rifle.

**Officials**  Men who ran the government.

**Opium**  A powerful drug made from poppies.

**Outback**  Remote parts of Australia.

**Pack animal**  An animal used to carry supplies.

**Pass**  A narrow passage through the mountains.

**Provisions**  Supplies for an expedition, especially food.

**Quinine**  A medicine that helps to cure malaria.

**Scoop**  An exclusive news story.

**Scout**  Someone who goes out in search of information.

**Scurvy**  A disease caused by lack of vitamins. Symptoms include internal bleeding and loosing teeth.

**Settlements**  Scattered groups of people living in the outback.

**Stamina**  Energy to keep doing something for a long period of time.

**Transcontinental**  Stretching right across the continent.

**Treaty**  A peace agreement.

**Tsar**  An emperor, like a king.

**Viceroy**  A governor appointed to rule India by the British government.

**Workhouse**  A place where poor people could live and be fed in return for work they did within the house.

# FURTHER INFORMATION

**Books to Read**

Arnold, Nick, *Voyages of Exploration: Quest,* (Wayland, 1995)
Beattie, Owen and Geiger, John, *Buried in Ice,* (Hodder and Stoughton/Madison Press, 1992)
Everett, Felicity and Reid, Struan, *The Usborne Book of Explorers: From Columbus to Armstrong,* (Usborne, 1991).
Draper, R. and Bull, P., *Explorers and Voyages of Discovery,* (Watts, 1993).
Humble, Richard, *Expeditions of Amundsen,* (Watts, 1991).
Humble, Richard, *Travels of Livingstone,* (Watts, 1991).
MacDonald, Fiona, *Explorers: Timelines* (Watts, 1994).
Rogers, Daniel, *Famous Explorers,* (Wayland, 1993).
Tames, Richard, *Great Explorers: What Happened Next?* (Watts, 1995).

For older readers:
*The Guiness Book of Explorers and Exploration,* edited by Michele Gavet-Imbert (Guiness, 1991)

**Places to Visit**

David Livingstone Centre, 165 Station Road, Blantyre, Lanarkshire G72 9BT. Tel: 01698 823140.

Denbigh Castle Museum, Denbigh, Flintshire. Tel: 01745 713979. The cottage where Sir Henry Morton Stanley was born lies just below the castle walls.

McDouall Stuart Museum, Rectory Lane, Dysart, Fife. Tel: 01592 260732.

Totnes Elizabethan Museum, 70 Fore Street, Totnes, Devon TQ9 5RU. Tel: 01803 863821.
This museum has a special section devoted to John Wills, who was born in Totnes.

# INDEX

Africa 4–8, 9–23, 43, 44
Amundsen, Roald 30
Arctic 24–30
Australia 31–4

Baker, Sir Samuel and Lady
  Florence 23
Beechy Island 24
Brahe, William 32–3
British Empire 9, 35
Burke, Robert O'Hara 9, 32–4
Burton, Richard 9, 22

Congo River 21
Coopers Creek 32–4
Curzon, Lord 35, 37, 38

Dalai Lama 38, 40
Dorijev, Arguan 38, 41

*Erebus* 24, 27, 28, 29
Eyre, John 31

Flinders, Matthew 31
*Fox* 29, 30
Franklin, Sir John 9, 24–30

*Gjoa* 30
Gobi Desert 36
Great Game 35–42
Great Zimbabwe 7
Guru 40

Henry the Navigator 6
Himalayas 35, 38

India 6, 35, 36
*Investigator* 28

Kalahari Desert 14, 15
King, John 33–4

Kolobeng 13
Kuruman 12, 13

*Lady Alice* 20
Lake Albert 23
Lake Bangweulu 19
Lake Ngami 14
Lake Nyasa 17, 18
Lake Tanganyika 4, 18, 20
Lake Victoria 20, 21
Leichhardt, Ludwig 31
Lhasa 38, 41, 42
Livingstone, Dr David 4–5, 8, 9,
  10–18, 22, 43
London Missionary Society 11,
  16
Lualaba River 20, 21

malaria 14, 18
Mandela, Nelson 44
Merowe 7
Moffat, Dr Robert 11, 12

Nile River 19, 20, 21, 22, 23

Point Victory 29

quinine 14, 17, 20

Royal Geographical Society 9
Royal Navy 24, 26, 29
Russian Empire 35

slave trade 4, 6, 7, 17, 19, 44
Speke, John Hanning 9, 22
Stanley, Sir Henry Morton 5, 9,
  18, 19, 20–1
Stuart, John McDouall 34
Sturt, Charles 31

*Terror* 24, 27, 28

Tibet 35, 37, 38–42
Torrington, John 24, 25

Ujiji 4, 5, 11, 18

Victoria Falls 16

Wills, John 9, 32–4

Younghusband, Sir Francis 9,
  35–7, 38

Zambezi River 15, 17